The
Rainy day
Book

Jane Bull

DK

DK Publishing

A Penguin Company
LONDON, NEW YORK, MUNICH,
MELBOURNE, AND DELHI

DESIGN • Jane Bull
EDITOR • Penelope Arlon
PHOTOGRAPHY • Andy Crawford
DESIGN ASSISTANCE • Sadie Thomas

MANAGING EDITOR • Sue Leonard
MANAGING ART EDITOR • Clare Shedden
PRODUCTION • Shivani Pandey
DTP DESIGNER • Almudena Díaz

For Charlotte, Billy, and James

First American Edition, 2003

Published in the United States by
DK Publishing, Inc.
375 Hudson Street
New York, New York 10014

03 04 05 06 07 08 10 9 8 7 6 5 4 3 2 1

Library of Congress Cataloging-in-Publication Data
Bull, Jane, 1957-
  The rainy day book / by Jane Bull.-- 1st American ed.
    p. cm. -- (Jane Bull's things to make and do)
Summary: Suggests a variety of crafts and activities using
common household materials, such as creating board games,
making pop-up books, doing origami, and several different things
that can be done with a potato.
  ISBN 0-7894-9831-6 (hardcover)
  1. Handicraft--Juvenile literature. [1. Handicraft.] I. Title. II.
Series.
  TT160.B863 2003
  745.5--dc21
                                    2003003565

ISBN: 0-7894-9831-6

Color reproduction by GRB Editrice S.r.l., Verona, Italy
Printed and bound in Italy by L.E.G.O.

Discover more at
www.dk.com

OK!
load it up

Prepare to keep out the
rainy day gloom

Bright ideas for a rainy day . . .

weave away the gloom...

...and pour out some fun

Rainy day survival kit

Be prepared! Collect bits and pieces regularly, like the things all around this page, so that when it rains, you have lots to work with.

Look for Bob on this page
Find out who he is on page 44

Materials and tools used in the book

Felt-tip pens • Plain paper • Face paints and sponges
• Paintbrushes • Wallpaper paste • Glue
• Scraps of material • Knitting and sewing needles
• Scissors • String • Yarn • All kinds of paper
• Buttons and beads • Materials to cook with

How to Survive a
Rainy Day

The rain is pouring down and there's simply nowhere to go. What are you going to do? You could watch television OR you could have some fun.

Why not feast on cookies, take a dot for a walk, say "hello" to your hands, get wrapped up in string—and if it's still raining after all that, you can try catching it!

Rainy day doodles

You won't believe what you can do with a doodle! Just put the pen down on the page and wave and wriggle away. Let your pen run free!

Take a dot for a walk

and color in the spaces

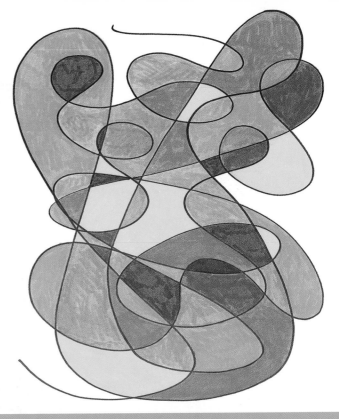

Lines and loops

It may look complicated, but that's the fun of it. It's easy!
Draw straight lines across the paper, then draw a loopy
shape over the top. Now color in alternate shapes.

Take a dot for another walk

Put your pen down and let your hand move freely across
a page. Feel free to cross lines and cut up circles. Now
color in each shape and watch the pattern come to life.

Eye-boggling spiral

Draw lots of circles from the center, each getting bigger,
then draw lines outward, like a web. Color them in.

weaving waves

Draw wavy lines acoss the page and down. Then
color in alternate squares for bulging patterns.

Hello, hands!

Forget your face, paint your hands instead! Turn your fingers into little personalities.

Face paints

Water for thinning paint.

Fine and thick brushes, and a washable felt-tip pen.

Sponges to paint large areas.

wet the sponge and dab it in the paint.

Paint your hand all over with the sponge.

Add the details with a paintbrush.

Soccer crazy

Let's go!

My ball

Yes!

Hints and tips

• Choose a good-quality face paint.
• Look at your hands and decide on a shape that suits your fingers.
• Use a damp sponge to cover large areas. Wait for it to dry before you paint the details.
• Use a washable felt-tip for outlines and faces.
• Clean the paints off with soap and water.

Pretty Polly

Creatures with beaks and long necks work well, too, like this parrot. Try other birds—a rooster or a pink flamingo.

Elephant fingers

I am an alien

I liked the sliding tackle. Good game, Jim!

Paper pots

There's paper all around you. Don't throw it away, recycle it!

Candy wrappers

Colored foil

Envelopes

Colored paper

Comics

Magazines

Newspaper

How to make a pot

Vaseline

1. Blow up a balloon, spread it with Vaseline, brush over some paste, and cover it with paper.

See page 46 for more about paste.

Wallpaper paste

2. Cover it with about six layers. Leave it to dry in a warm place.

3. Take the balloon out and trim off the rough edges.

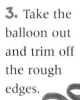

4. Make a base from a strip of cardboard, tape it on. Cover it with paste and paper.

5. Cut out cardboard ears, tape them on, and cover with paste and paper.

Decorate inside and out.

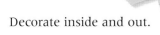

Box rooms
where your toys can live. Decorate and furnish them with odds and ends

Find a cardboard box

Measure the paper

Use wrapping paper or paint your own wallpaper.

Draw and cut out windows

⭐ **Ask an adult** to help cut the thick card.

You will need
For the house itself:
- A cardboard box
- Scissors, ruler, and pen
- Decorated wallpaper
- Material for the carpet
- Glue

Decorate the walls

Glue the wallpaper to the inside of the box.

Cover the floor

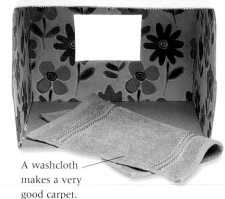

A washcloth makes a very good carpet.

Ahh, home, sweet home

Come in out of the rain

All I need now is a comfy chair

How to make scrap furniture

Collect boxes, cartons, and other bits and pieces that are going to be thrown away—imagine how many you will gather over the weeks for those rainy days. You'll have a great collection.

Small boxes

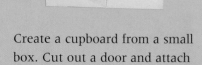

Create a cupboard from a small box. Cut out a door and attach a split pin handle onto it.

Lamp

Stick a straw in a spool of thread and pop a muffin case on top.

Popsicle sticks

Ice cream cone

Armchair

Paint four matchboxes and glue them together.

Clothes-peg

Matchboxes

Bottle lid

Table

Stick a large lid onto a drinks bottle lid with a piece of modelling clay.

Modelling clay

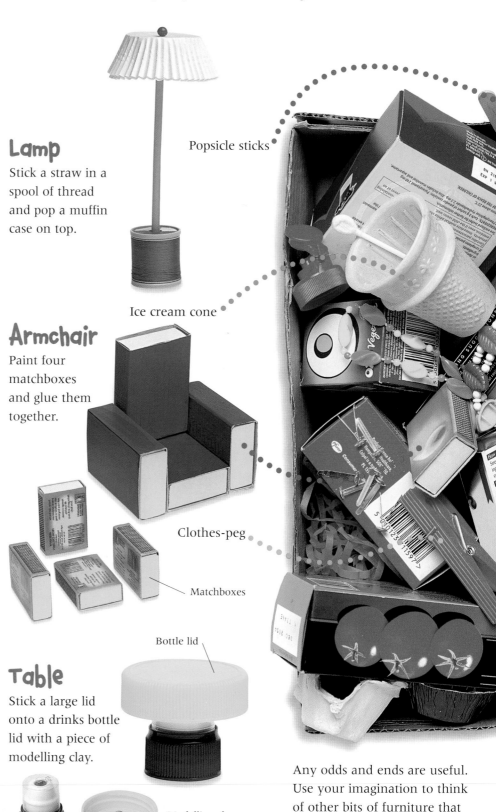

Any odds and ends are useful. Use your imagination to think of other bits of furniture that can go inside your box room.

You will need

- Odds and ends from around the house.
- Adhesive tape
- Paper fasteners
- Paint and brushes
- Modelling clay
- Paper fasteners
- Glue

Straws

Cut two slits into a cardboard box and push the center through.

Comfy chair

Stick a matchbox onto the bigger box.

Cardboard tubes

Beads

Plant

Pop some modelling clay into a plastic lid and stick in some beads.

Beads and buttons

Cover the drawers with bright paper.

Paper fastener

Drawers

Three matchboxes and paper fasteners.

Plastic spoon

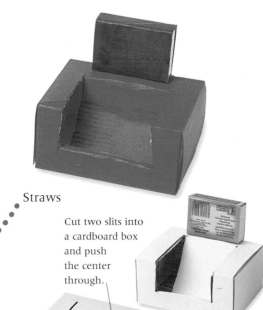

Lids and caps

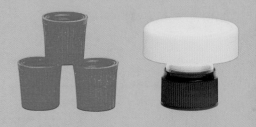

Lids from empty tubes of paint make tiny cups or plant pots. Lids and caps can be made into tiny tables.

Pets' corner

Create cages for your furry toys—
open your very own animal hospital.

You will need
- A cardboard box
- Glue, tape
- Scissors
- Paper fasteners
- Black pen

Cozy hutch

Help your cuddly pets feel right at home by cutting strips of scrap paper for their bed. Give them food and water bowls, and every so often, let them out for a cuddle. The good thing about toy pets is that you never need to clean up after them!

Draw swirls with a black pen on the cardboard to make it look like wood.

Cage door

Make a cage door for your hutch out of cardboard. Measure your box and cut two long cardboard strips and two shorter pieces.

The long pieces must be about 2 in (6 cm) longer than the length of the box.

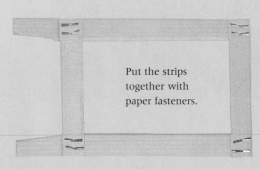

Put the strips together with paper fasteners.

Make sure that it fits exactly onto the outside of the box.

It's feeding time!

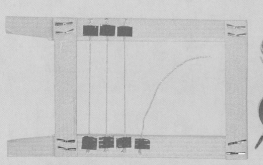

Use yarn for the cage bars by sticking
pieces to the top and bottom of the back.

Attach the cage
door by gluing the
flaps to the side of
the box, or use paper
fasteners instead.

Use cardboard
and a split
pin for
a latch.

17

Salt dough

Four activities in one

1. Mixing
2. Modeling
3. Cooking
4. Painting

Mix the dough and squeeze it into any shape you like, for hours of doughy fun.

To make the dough

You will need

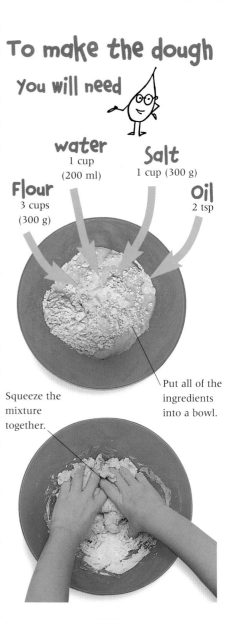

water
1 cup
(200 ml)

Salt
1 cup (300 g)

Flour
3 cups
(300 g)

Oil
2 tsp

Put all of the ingredients into a bowl.

Squeeze the mixture together.

Pat it into a ball.

Roll it out

Now have fun!

Make a good impression

Play with your dough

Roll it, rake it, squash it, squeeze it. Look around your house for objects to press into the dough. You can create all kinds of effects and shapes, and if you don't like them, roll them up and start over.

If the dough gets sticky, sprinkle on some flour.

20

Bear necessities

Make the bear shapes.

Stick them together.

Squash a paperclip onto the back.

Bake the bear, then paint it.

Tie on a ribbon.

Baking your shapes

Place your shapes on a baking tray.

If the shapes are big, they will take longer to cook, and if they are delicate, they may break more easily, so keep them small and chunky.

Let them cool down before you paint them.

☆ **Ask an adult** to help with the oven.

Bake for 20 minutes at 350°F (180°C)

Painting and decorating

When the baked dough has cooled down, you can paint it with poster or acrylic paint. Try mixing a little PVA glue to the paint (about 1 part PVA to 2 parts paint)—this will make it tough and shiny.

More about PVA glue on page 46.

Keeping your dough

You can save your unbaked dough by covering it in plastic wrap. It will keep for about two weeks.

Save it for a rainy day

21

Sweet dough

Dough you can eat – make these tasty shortbread cookies.

Flour

Butter

Sugar

Yum Yum

Roll the dough into a ball and squash it flat.

Squash with a fork

Cookie Dough

Makes 12-16 plain cookies
2½ cups (250 g) flour
¾ cup (150 g) butter
½ cup (90 g) sugar

Put the flour, sugar, and butter into a bowl.
Squeeze them together with your fingers until they come together to make a ball of dough.
Shape your biscuits and decorate them.
Place them on a baking tray.
Cook for 15 minutes at 325ºF (160ºC)
Cool them on a cooling rack and DIG IN!

For chocolate biscuits:
2½ cups (250 g) flour
⅓ cup (30 g) cocoa powder
¾ cup (150 g) butter
½ cup (90 g) sugar

For coconut biscuits:
Add ⅔ cup (60 g) shredded coconut to the mix.

Ask an adult to help with the oven.

Leave some space between your cookies.

Making patterns

Try jimmies and colorful candies for decoration, or use plain and chocolate dough together to create spots and stripes.

Jimmies

Chocolate chips

Coconut

Candies

Big chocolate candies

On your mark, get set... Line up your toys, stack up the blocks...

use the furniture

It will give extra height to the ramps.

Grrrr!

24

ready for the Domino Run? Go!

A spectacular run

Push the car at the top of the stool and watch it go! Set up the dominoes so that as one falls, it will knock down the next, and so on. The aim is to create a set that will fall from beginning to end without stopping.

You will need

- Dominoes
- Boxes
- Cardboard tubes
- Building blocks
- Bits and pieces to help the run.

what will happen? Turn to page 43

Get weaving

wonderful webs in rainbow colors.

Paper plate

yarn

A paper plate and scraps of yarn create a rainbow web to brighten up your day.

To weave a web
You will need
- A paper plate or posterboard disk
- Scraps of yarn
- Darning needle

26

1

Draw out a zig-zag edge around the plate and cut out the triangles.

2

See page 46 for other ways to start off.

knot

Loop the yarn around two opposite spikes, making sure they cross in the middle, and tie a kot in the center.

3

Keep crossing the yarn from spike to spike, making sure the yarn crosses through the middle.

The yarn will go around this one next.

4

Keep going backward and forward across the plate.

5

Turn your plate over and it should look like this. Tie the end of the yarn into a knot.

6

Thread a piece of yarn onto a needle. From the middle, weave the needle between the strands.

It will look strange at first, but after about six rows, it will even out.

7

As you weave, make sure you pull the yarn tight into the middle

8

Knot a new piece of yarn to the last one and just keep on weaving.

use up your old scraps

Continue weaving in different colors until there's no more room.

keep on weaving

Looms are frames used for weaving fabric. Make a simple loom and try creating a piece of fabric—and then start to weave anything you can find!

Homemade loom

A shoebox lid is ideal. Cut the same number of slits on opposite ends, then thread yarn backward and forward.

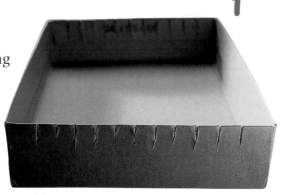

1

⭐ **Ask an adult** to cut the slits—they may need to use a sharp knife.

2

Wrap the yarn around the first slit to hold it in place.

3

Keep going up and down.

4

Thread the yarn above and below the main strands and forward and back.

Now try weaving other things that you can find.

5

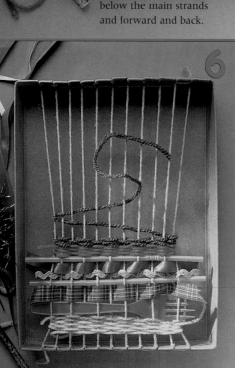

Weave and weave until you reach the top.

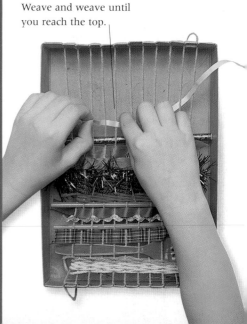

6

A work of weaving art - hang it on the wall for all to see.

Ribbon

Yarn

Plastic
Knife

Pencil

Tinsel

Straw

Fancy
Ribbon

Plastic
Fork

Scrap bags

These floppy bag people

are made from scraps of left-
over material and filled
with dried beans.

"Try me, I'm
very filling!"
yell the lentils.

Play with us, we're full of beans!

Throw together a scrap bag

**Here,
catch!**

To make a bag
Use the scrap bag pattern to measure the size of your bag. Cut out a piece of fabric and fold it in half.

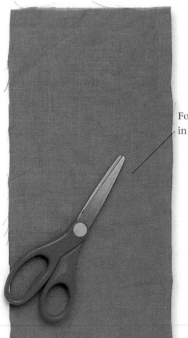

Fold it
in half.

LEAVE A HOLE

STITCHING LINE

Scrap bag pattern
Follow this
pattern to help
you with the size.

FOLD THE FABRIC HERE

STITCHING LINE

LEAVE A HOLE

Leave an opening at the top.

Back stitch around the open sides.

Turn the bag inside out.

Fill it with dried peas or beans.

To finish it off, stitch up the hole at the top.

Pin it together   **Sew up the sides**   **Turn inside out and fill up**   **Close it up**

Back stitch

A good stitch to use is back stitch, because it completely seals the sides. Don't be fooled into thinking you can do a simple running stitch— if you do, the beans will fall out!

See page 46 for back stitch instructions.

Sew or use PVA glue to stick on the faces.

Scrap bag games

Target practice

Set up a target area around a bucket and challenge your family to score high. Make up the rules yourself!

Juggling

Start with two, then build up your bags. A perfect practice for a rainy day.

Play catch

Throw a bag for a friend to catch. If they miss, they go down on one knee; miss again, they go down on two knees; and so on, until they are lying down.

Bad luck! To score 100, it has to go right into the bowl.

100

50

25

Good shot! that's 100 points!

String things

All wound up! From see-through string balls to fluffy pom-pons, there's a whole new woolly world to discover.

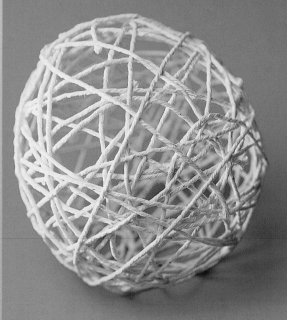

Juggle those pom-pons!

How to make a string thing

You will need • Balloon • String or yarn • Wallpaper paste • Vaseline

Blow up a balloon and spread Vaseline all over it to keep the string from sticking to the balloon.

Mix up a bowl of wallpaper paste.

Cut some pieces of string, about 22 in (60 cm) long.

Inflated balloon

Wallpaper paste

Vaseline

String

Dip the string into the paste, then wrap it around the balloon.

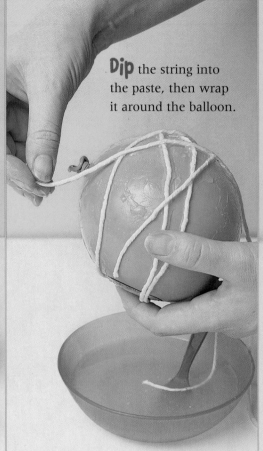

Watch out!
This part gets messy

Add more and more and more string until you have enough.

Leave it to dry overnight

How to make a pom-pon

You will need • Thin cardboard • Yarn

Tip: The larger the disks, the bigger your pom-pon will turn out.

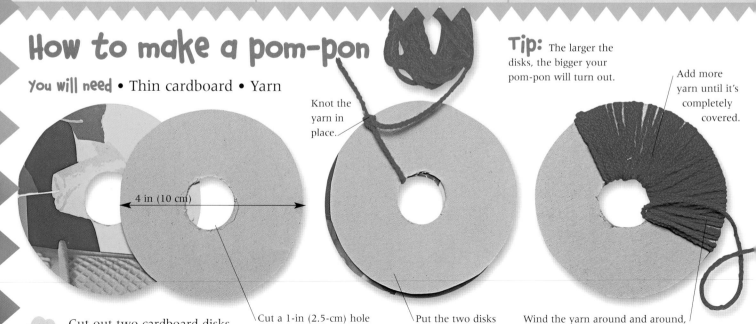

Knot the yarn in place.

Add more yarn until it's completely covered.

4 in (10 cm)

Cut out two cardboard disks.

Cut a 1-in (2.5-cm) hole in the middle of each disk.

Put the two disks together.

Wind the yarn around and around, through the middle and over the top.

When the string is dry...

pop the balloon!

Put the scissors between the two disks.

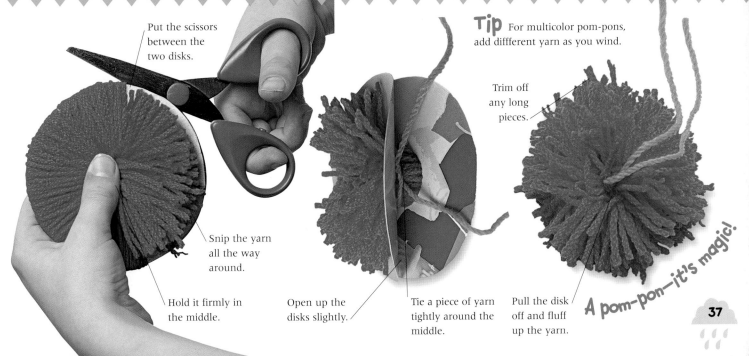

Tip For multicolor pom-pons, add diffferent yarn as you wind.

Trim off any long pieces.

Snip the yarn all the way around.

Hold it firmly in the middle.

Open up the disks slightly.

Tie a piece of yarn tightly around the middle.

Pull the disk off and fluff up the yarn.

A pom-pon—it's magic!

why not make a friendship
bracelet for your favorite friend?

Knitting

Master the skill of knitting. Begin with your fingers and thumbs and work up to needles. As well as yarn, you will need lots of patience, so DON'T give up.

Finger knitting

This is also called finger crochet. Wind the yarn around your thumb twice, then pick up the first loop and take it over the second. Keep repeating this until it has grown to the length you want.

It's growing

1 Wind the yarn around your thumb twice.

2 Pick up the first loop.

3 Take it over the second loop.

4 Keep going.

5 Carefully pull the yarn.

6 Pull the yarn so the stitch is secure on your finger.

7 Repeat the steps. The first loop is there, so wind the yarn to make the second.

Use two pieces of different-colored yarn to make a multicolored wristband.

As you repeat the steps, the bracelet will grow and grow.

Knit a blanket

Once you have the hang of finger
knitting, you will have a good
idea how to cast on to needles
and start knitting. Using plain
stitch, you can make a finger
puppet from a single square, and
if you get really ambitious, you
can make lots of squares
to make a blanket.

I'm in
stitches!

How to knit

Follow these knitting instructions and you'll be using plain stitch with standard needles. Once you get the hang of it, there'll be no stopping you—you'll be well and truly hooked!

You will need
- Knitting needles, size 6 (4 mm)
- Ball of yarn

Casting on – this is how you get the stitches onto the needle.

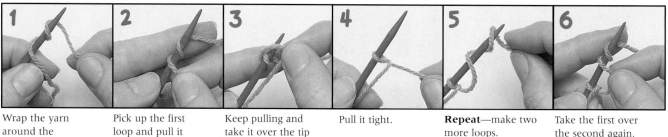

1 Wrap the yarn around the needle twice.

2 Pick up the first loop and pull it over the second.

3 Keep pulling and take it over the tip of the needle.

4 Pull it tight.

5 **Repeat**—make two more loops.

6 Take the first over the second again.

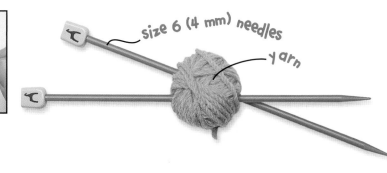

size 6 (4 mm) needles

yarn

7 Keep pulling it tight as you go.

8 Take it right over the needle again, as before.

9 Keep repeating this until you have 12 stitches.

Plain stitch

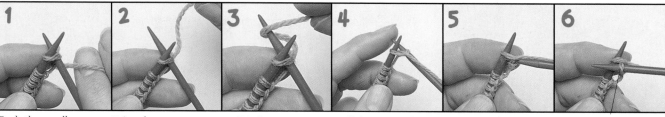

1 Push the needle through the front of the first stitch.

2 Bring the yarn around the back of the needles.

3 Pull it down between them.

4 Pull the yarn tight.

5 Bring the needle back up, with the loop still attached, to form the stitch.

6 The stitch is now made.

7 Release the stitch onto the empty needle.

8 Repeat from step 1 to make the next stitch.

9 Push the needle in the front of the next stitch.

10 Bring the yarn around the back of the needles.

11 Pull it tight between the needles.

12 Push the needle down to make the stitch.

13 Bring the needle back and to the front again.

14 You now have two stitches.

15 Keep doing this until you finish the row.

The second stitch is now made.

Keep going!

Repeat these steps until you reach the length you want.

Casting off – do this when you have reached the length you want.

1 Knit two stitches.

2 Pull the first stitch over the second.

3 Let it go so there is one stitch on the needle.

4 Knit a new stitch.

5 Now you have two stitches on the needle.

6 Pull the first stitch over the second.

7 Continue reducing stitches until there is one left.

8 Make the last stitch big enough to tie a knot.

9 Snip off the yarn.

10 Put it through the loop and pull it tight.

11 Snip off the excess yarn.

well done, you've made it!

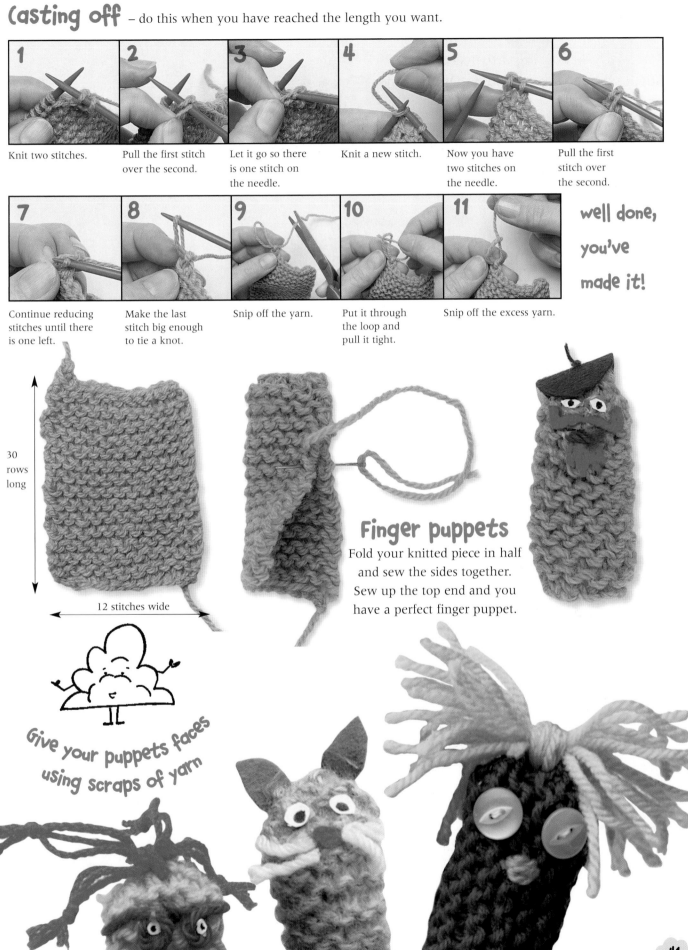

30 rows long

12 stitches wide

Finger puppets

Fold your knitted piece in half and sew the sides together. Sew up the top end and you have a perfect finger puppet.

Give your puppets faces using scraps of yarn

The domino effect

Now it's time to see what happens when you knock the first little car down the ramp. Watch out!

Tunnels and ramps can be made from cardboard tubes, either cut in half or whole.

Domino tip

Be very, very careful when you lay the dominoes out. If you make a mistake, you may have to start all over.

It's a complete mess!

It doesn't stop!

42

Away it goes!

The car hits the dominoes, the dominoes ram the car, and whoosh! it flies through the tunnel, straight into the people standing at the bottom!

Down the tube

Roar....yum, yum!

Chain reaction

Everything is all over the place. As one goes, the others follow— what a mess and what a noise!

Crash! It's over!

The grand finale

The dominoes crash into the truck, which rolls down the ramp, knocks into the tube carrying the strainer full of candies, which falls and… mmm! The dinosaur gets his meal!

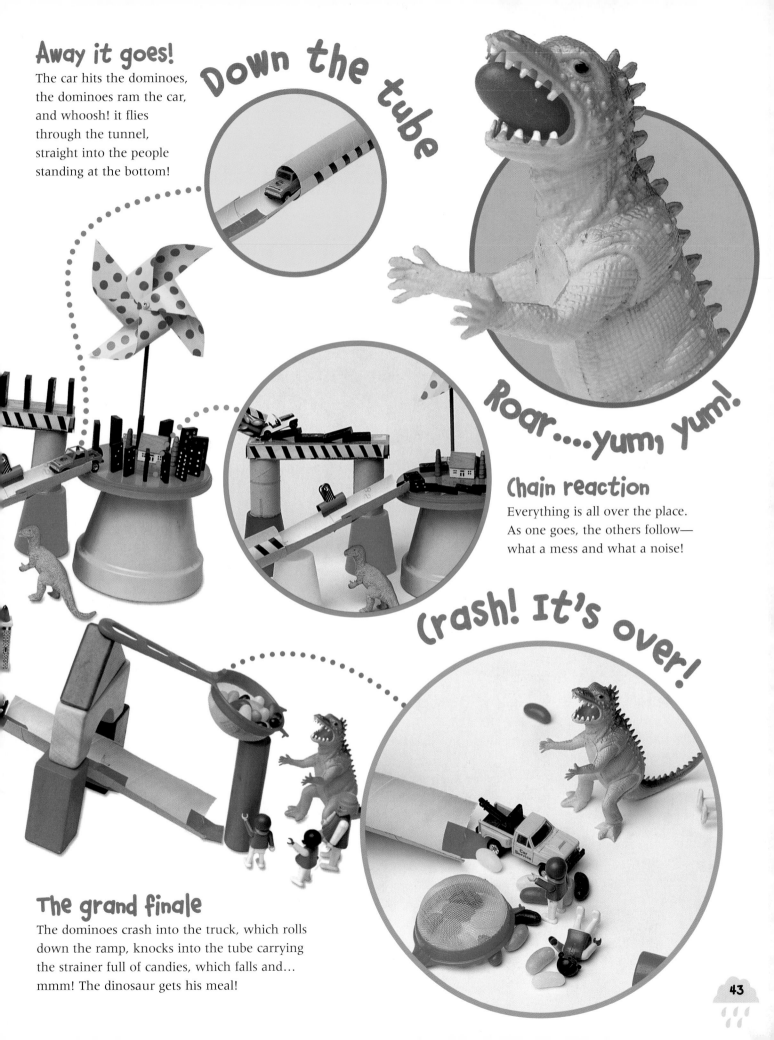

Activity centers – jars packed full of fun

Jars are perfect for filling with lots of little things for your craft projects. Alternatively, fill one up with games, such as dice and cards—useful for those rainy days.

Cards, counters, and quizzes

Beads, buttons, and ribbons

where's Bob?

A game of hide and seek

If you look carefully throughout this book, you will see Bob popping up on certain spreads. Have you seen him yet? The pages he is on are listed on page 48.

Come and get me!

Memory game

Look at these objects for 30 seconds. Now close the book and see how many you can remember. How did you score?

How many can you remember?

Try this on your family. Prepare a tray of objects. Let them study it for 30 seconds. **Time's up!** Quickly cover it up again. The person who can remember all the objects is the winner!

44

Take a potato and make...

Potato heads

Use buttons, cocktail sticks, hair clips, faces from magazines, or anything else you can think of to dress up your potatoes.

Pin the faces in place.

A potato pooch

Potato bake

Scrub and wash a potato. Put it straight in the oven set at 375°F (190°C). Bake for about an hour, or until it's soft inside. Take it out and fill it up with cheese.

Cheese and chives on the top.

Potato patterns

Don't put on too much paint.

Cut a potato in half and draw a shape on the inside with a felt-tip pen. Carefully cut it out with a knife—remember to cut around your design. Brush paint onto the surface and press it onto some paper.

Keep designs simple

Handy hints and tips

All about glue

Glue stick   Wallpaper paste   All-purpose glue

wallpaper paste

You can buy this paste in bags from any home improvement store. Put about a tablespoon of the flakes into a bowl and add water until it blends in. It should be thick enough to brush onto a surface.

Glue stick

This is a very clean glue and is best for paper, since it won't make it crinkle.

All-purpose glue

This is not only a strong glue, it also smells strong. Use it for gluing cardboard pieces together.

PVA glue (Elmer's glue)

PVA is very useful glue for fabric and cardboard. Mixed with a bit of water, it is a good varnish, and mixed with paint, it will give the colored surface a shiny finish.

Threading a needle

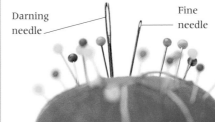

Darning needle   Fine needle

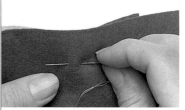

Push the fine wire through the eye.

This gadget helps you thread a needle. You can get them in any store that sells thread.

Push the needle down to the metal.

Thread your yarn through the wire.

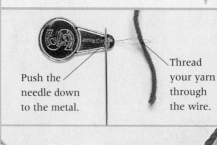

Now just pull the threader and the needle apart and you've done it—easy!

Keep on pulling, and then remove the wire threader.

Sewing backstitch

Knot the end of the thread and push the needle down and up through the fabric.

Pull the needle all the way through to the knot.

Place the needle between the knot and the dangling thread.

Bring the needle up ahead of the dangling thread.

Repeat these steps and sew over a few stitches to finish off.

Get weaving
(page 27)
Quick start and finish

If you have trouble getting your weaving started, use sticky tape to hold the wool in place.

Tape the yarn to the back of the plate.

Turn the plate over and wind the wool as on page 33.

When you are finished, turn the plate over.

Tape the other end.

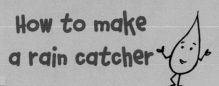

How to make a rain catcher

Take a plastic bottle—one with a flat bottom is the best.

Ask an Adult to help you cut the bottle.

Cut the bottle into two pieces as shown.

Turn the top over and place it back into the bottle base.

Make a dipstick from a wooden spoon. Measure and draw out $1/2$-in (1-cm) spaces with a pen.

Pop a drop of food coloring into the bottle so that you can see the water easily.

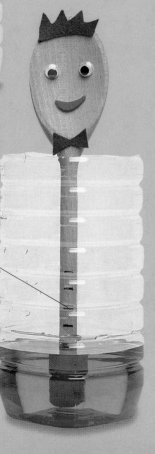

Rain catcher

Rain, rain, go away

If the rain won't go away, make yourself a gauge to measure just how much has fallen. Place some pebbles around the bottom to keep it stable, and check the depth each day against the dipstick.

Index

Did you spot Bob?

Look for him on pages:
4, 17, 24, 39, 42, 44, and 46.

Acknowledgments

With thanks to...
Maisie Armah, Charlotte Bull, Billy Bull,
James Bull, Luke Bower, and
Sorcha Lyons for performing the
projects on their rainy days off.

All images © Dorling Kindersley.
For further information see:
www.dkimages.com

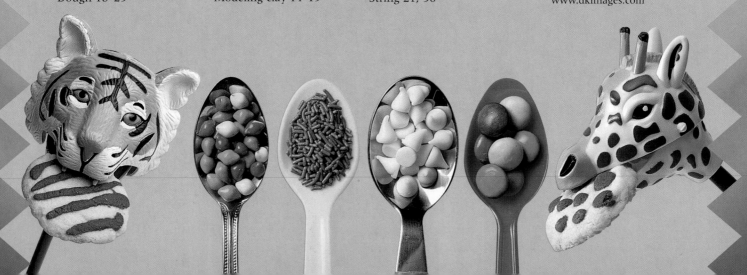